HAL•LEONARD
INSTRUMENTAL
PLAY-ALONG

AUDIO
ACCESS
INCLUDED

PLAYBACK+
Speed • Pitch • Balance • Loop

CLARINET

T0069305

Audio arrangements by Peter Deneff

To access audio, visit:
www.halleonard.com/mylibrary

"Enter Code"
3646-5874-5409-1916

ISBN 978-1-5400-9208-3

For all works contained herein:
Unauthorized copying, arranging, adapting, recording, Internet posting, public performance,
or other distribution of the music in this publication is an infringement of copyright.
Infringers are liable under the law.

Visit Hal Leonard Online at
www.halleonard.com

Contact us:
Hal Leonard
7777 West Bluemound Road
Milwaukee, WI 53213
Email: info@halleonard.com

In Europe, contact:
Hal Leonard Europe Limited
42 Wigmore Street
Marylebone, London, W1U 2RN
Email: info@halleonardeurope.com

In Australia, contact:
Hal Leonard Australia Pty. Ltd.
4 Lentara Court
Cheltenham, Victoria, 3192 Australia
Email: info@halleonard.com.au

CONTENTS

BAD GUY

Clarinet

Words and Music by BILLIE EILISH O'CONNELL
and FINNEAS O'CONNELL

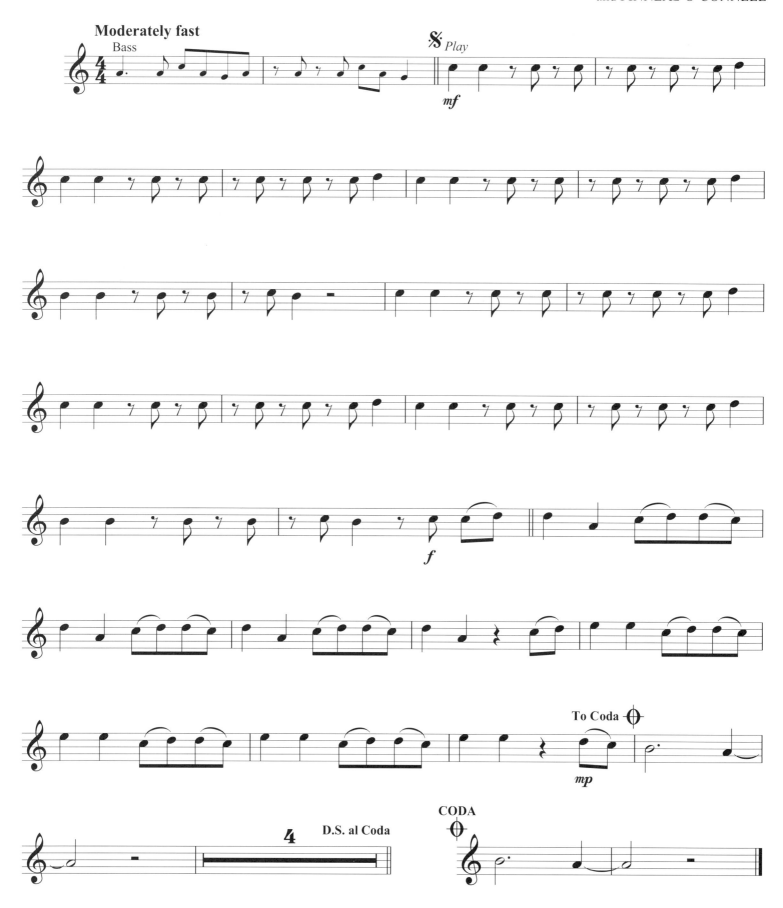

I LOVE YOU

Clarinet

Words and Music by BILLIE EILISH O'CONNELL
and FINNEAS O'CONNELL

EVERYTHING I WANTED

Clarinet

Words and Music by BILLIE EILISH O'CONNELL
and FINNEAS O'CONNELL

Idontwannabeyouanymore

CLARINET

Words and Music by BILLIE EILISH O'CONNELL
and FINNEAS O'CONNELL

LOVELY

CLARINET

Words and Music by BILLIE EILISH O'CONNELL,
FINNEAS O'CONNELL and KHALID ROBINSON

NO TIME TO DIE

Clarinet

Words and Music by BILLIE EILISH O'CONNELL
and FINNEAS O'CONNELL

OCEAN EYES

CLARINET

Words and Music by
FINNEAS O'CONNELL

YOU SHOULD SEE ME IN A CROWN

Clarinet

Words and Music by BILLIE EILISH O'CONNELL
and FINNEAS O'CONNELL

WHEN THE PARTY'S OVER

CLARINET

Words and Music by
FINNEAS O'CONNELL